What's an INSECT?

Anna Kaspar

PowerKiDS press.

New York

Published in 2012 by The Rosen Publishing Group, Inc.
29 East 21st Street, New York, NY 10010

First Edition

Editor: Amelie von Zumbusch
Book Design: Ashley Drago

Photo Credits: Cover © www.iStockphoto.com/Anyka; pp. 5, 10, 13, 18, 21, 24 (caterpillar, luna moth) Shutterstock.com; pp. 6, 24 (antennae) © www.iStockphoto.com/Imagedepotpro; p. 9 iStockphoto/Thinkstock; pp. 14, 24 (wasp) © www.iStockphoto.com/Arman Davtyan; p. 17 John Foxx/Stockbyte/Thinkstock; p. 22 Brian Gordon Green/Getty Images.

Library of Congress Cataloging-in-Publication Data

Kaspar, Anna.
  What's an insect? / by Anna Kaspar. — 1st ed.
     p. cm. — (All about animals)
  Includes index.
  ISBN 978-1-4488-6139-2 (library binding) — ISBN 978-1-4488-6236-8 (pbk.) — ISBN 978-1-4488-6237-5 (6-pack)
  1. Insects—Juvenile literature. I. Title.
  QL467.2.K366 2012
  595.7—dc23

                          2011023952

Manufactured in the United States of America

CPSIA Compliance Information: Batch #WW12PK: For Further Information contact Rosen Publishing, New York, New York at 1-800-237-9932

Contents

Insects are Earth's most common kind of animal.

Insects have **antennae** on their heads. Insects sense things with their antennae.

Adult insects have six legs. Their bodies have three parts.

9

Insects pass through stages as they grow. Butterflies start out as **caterpillars**.

Ants live in groups called colonies. The members of a colony live and work together.

Wasps often live in colonies, too. Most wasps eat other kinds of insects.

Bees drink from flowers. Some bees dance to show other bees where to find flowers.

18

Flies use the hairs on their feet to taste things.

Luna moths live in North America. Females make a smell that draws males to them.

Male crickets chirp. They rub their wings together to make noise.

WORDS TO KNOW

antennae

caterpillar

luna moth

wasp

INDEX

WEB SITES

Due to the changing nature of Internet links, PowerKids Press has developed an online list of Web sites related to the subject of this book. This site is updated regularly. Please use this link to access the list: www.powerkidslinks.com/aaa/insect/